betterkids

# my MEDITATIONS with WISDOM



based on the game

Wisdom: The World of Emotions

www.betterkids.education

"Close your eyes and find stillness as you prepare your minds to focus on the journey ahead..."

# MY MEDITATIONS

Whether you are feeling anxious, angry, unmotivated, or sad,
these meditations were made especially for you!
They will help you feel calm and grounded in the present
moment. Choose your favorite quiet place to read the
meditations to yourself or ask an adult to read-aloud for you.
Use the reflection questions and Meditation Journals to help
you remember how the meditation made you feel.

Remember your emotions are unique to you!

# Table of Contents

Meditations are perfect to use for morning meetings, helping with transitions, or at the end of the day.

Here are some tips on how to use these meditations at school:

• Some meditations may require children to be sitting in a chair. For the other meditations children should be sitting in a comfortable position, whether in a chair or on a carpet.

• You can set up a "peace corner" in your classroom with a comfortable chair, a plant and by a window if possible where students can read the meditations independently or listen to recordings of them. You can create your own recordings or use the ones found in our app Wisdom: The World of Emotions.

• If your students take a nap, these meditations may also be helpful when they first lie down.

• Meditations should be read in a calm, soothing voice. If your students are reading, they can take turns reading the meditations aloud to the class, practicing pauses and talking softly.

Virtual Learning
• If you are a teacher and you notice your students are feeling anxious or are expressing other big emotions during virtual learning, a guided mediation may be a helpful activity. Each meditation can be read while the students are sitting. Make sure they are in a quiet space with few distractions if possible, and read the meditations in a soothing voice.

# At Home

After introducing the meditations to your child, they may find them to be a helpful coping tool for when they are feeling upset or anxious. Here are some tips for how to use these meditations at home:

• If your child is not yet reading, you can remind them you can read the meditation to them when they need help with feeling calm.

• Guided meditations are great to read together in a calming tone before bedtime.

• You can set up a "peace corner" in your home or your child's bedroom with a comfortable chair, a plant and by a window if possible where your child can read the meditations independently or listen to recordings of them. You can create your own recordings or use the ones found in our app Wisdom: The World of Emotions.

• Video call with grandparents, cousins, or friends: Your child can read the meditation to their loved one or you can gift loved ones with a copy of this book for them to read to your child!

• On the Wisdom: The World of Emotions app: Your child can follow along in the book as Wisdom reads the meditations.

## You are the sun

*In this meditation your child will imagine themselves as the sun, full of warmth, brightness, and confidence. This meditation is helpful for when your child needs to feel confident and motivated.*

Close your eyes and take a slow deep breath. Once you have found stillness in your body continue to take slow, deep breaths focusing on the pattern of your heartbeat and your breath.

Notice your inner energy. How does it feel? Are you calm or excited? Your energy radiates like the sun sharing its warmth with everyone it touches. You are the sun.

The sun nurtures plants with its energy, helping them to grow strong and full of life. Your energy nourishes those around you, your compassion helps them to feel strong and your joy fills others with liveliness. You are the sun.

Think about all the love that has been given to you and the love you have for them. Do you feel the warmth of their love in your heart? Just as the sun warms the heart, our love for each other warms our hearts. You are the sun.

Sometimes it is cloudy and it is harder to see the sun but we always know it is there. Even though there may be times you feel far away from others they can feel your presence. You are the sun.

As you take a deep breath in, imagine the sun slowly rising. When you wake in the morning imagine your energy brightening just as the colors of the sun brighten reaching everyone it touches with its new light. As you breathe out, imagine the sun slowly sinking back down, its waning light leaving a comforting reminder of its return the next day. Your brightness also returns with each new day. You are the sun.

Take some time to breathe in and out, enjoying the stillness just as the sun enjoys its midday rise high in the sky. When you are ready, open your eyes and observe the light in our presence.

## REFLECTION QUESTIONS

How has someone shown you love?

How have you shown love to someone?

Something that fills you with love and excitement is

## Flower breathing

*This meditation has your child focusing on a flower, its details, and taking deep breaths. This meditation is helpful for when your child is feeling anxious.*

First, find a comfortable sitting position.

Now sit up a little taller, so your chest is out and your heart feels big.

Put one hand in front of you and make a fist. Now put up just your pointer finger.

Imagine your finger is a flower. Think about how you want your flower to look. Look closely... What color is it? Is it a dark blue, like the sky at night? Is it white like a fluffy cloud? Is your flower orange like a sunset? Or is it some other color?

Imagine exactly how you would like your flower to look.

Now bring your finger a little closer to your face, but don't touch it. Breathe in through your nose, like you are trying to gently smell your flower. And breathe out. Imagine your lovely flower's smell. And when you breathe out, feel your breath on the flower like a gentle breeze. Keep breathing in and out. Smelling the flower with your nose, filling your lungs. Slowly breathing out a gentle wind from your mouth to the flower's stem.

Now close your eyes and continue breathing. Breathe in the smell of your flower. Breathe out and feel the wind on the flower. Feel your belly get big when you breathe in, and feel it shrink when you breathe out.

Continue taking a few more flower breaths on your own.

When you are ready, slowly open your eyes and take one more look at your flower. Remember what it looks like, so the next time you want to feel peaceful and calm, you can pull it out for more flower breathing.

## REFLECTION QUESTIONS

Who adds color to your life? Write the name of someone on each flower petal who knows how to make you smile.

Who helps hold you up when you are sad, scared, or discouraged? Write their name next to the flower stem.

Who provides you with nourishment? Write the name of someone on each leaf who makes sure you always feel filled with positivity.

Roots help flowers stay grounded so they can grow strong. Who are some other people in your life that support you and help you feel grounded? In what ways do you feel supported by them?

..............................................................................

## Seated meditation

*A good beginning guided meditation for children to think about how their bodies are positioned while practicing. This is a helpful meditation if your child is feeling anxious or overwhelmed.*



Close your eyes.

Sit in your chair so your back is against the chair's back. Position your feet so your toes are pointed forward. Feel your feet planted firmly on the ground, as if the entire bottom of your foot is glued to the floor. Imagine the ground and your feet hugging.

Now think about your back. Sit up tall and straight. Roll your shoulders back three times now with me. One. Two. Three. Great, now keep your shoulders back and relaxed down, far away from your ears. Imagine there are strings connected from the ground to your shoulders, and the strings are gently pulling your shoulders down.

Now think about your hands. Place them in your lap with your palms up. Think of all the light, fluffy air your hands are holding. Wiggle your fingers to feel the air. Then let your fingers fall open again, gently letting air rest in your hands.

Lift your chin, so your face is slightly toward the sky, eyes still closed.

Feel your chest and heart open up, so your chest is also facing slightly toward the sky. Let's take five deep breaths together, thinking about air coming in through your nostrils, into your lungs, and into your stomach, before leaving your mouth. Breathe in... feel air passing through your nostrils... and out. Breathe in... feel your chest grow... and out. Breathe in... feel your belly grow... and out. Breath in... and out. Breath in... and out.

Can you feel your heart beating? Can you hear it? Take a few slow breaths and listen for your heart beat.

When you are ready, flutter your eyes open.

## REFLECTION QUESTIONS

One obstacle I faced was when ..............................................

I overcame this obstacle by ..............................................

A few of my strengths are ..............................................

..............................................

..............................................

## Your favorite place

*This meditation has your child focusing on their favorite place and the emotions they feel thinking about this place. This is a helpful meditation for when your child is feeling angry or anxious.*

Close your eyes and take a deep breath in and a deep breath out. Slowly, take a few more deep breaths until you feel yourself relax as you find stillness in your body.

As you continue with your breathing rhythm, imagine in your mind your favorite place. Imagine you are present in this place you love right now. Think about all of the reasons why you love this place. Imagine every detail about what makes this place your favorite. Let this thought wrap around you like a warm hug.

Now, imagine someone there with you in your favorite place. Who did you think of? Have you been to this place with them before? Think about a memory you had or would like to have with this person there.

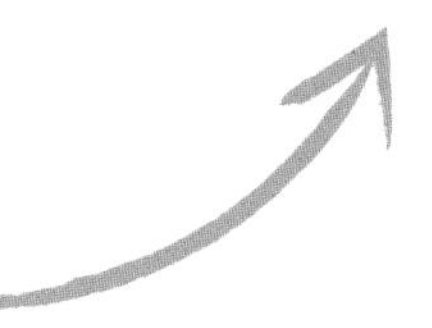

Think about the emotions you feel being in this place. Do you feel happiness in your heart? Are you smiling when you are in this place? Take a few moments to listen to what you might hear in your favorite place.

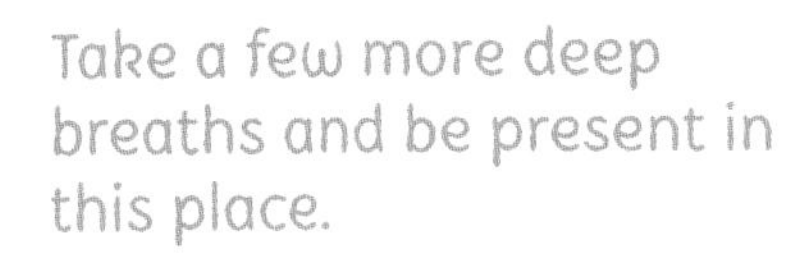

Take a few more deep breaths and be present in this place.

When you are ready, slowly open your eyes and observe your surroundings.

## REFLECTION QUESTIONS

Describe the place you were thinking of during this meditation using your five senses:

........................................................................................................

........................................................................................................

How did you feel thinking about your favorite place?

........................................................................................................

........................................................................................................

## Breathing like an ocean

*In this meditation your child will imagine they are the ocean as they take deep breaths. This is a helpful meditation if your child is feeling angry or overwhelmed.*

Close your eyes and find stillness in your body. Now, imagine you are the ocean. The sun is shining on you, the sky is blue, and there is a slight breeze nudging fluffy clouds along in the sky.

When we inhale through the nose, waves are forming, when we exhale through the mouth those waves come crashing on the shore.

Let's do three calm and peaceful waves taking slow breaths in through the nose and out through the mouth.

One... two... three...

Now imagine bigger waves and take a long, deep breath in through the nose and out through the mouth.
Let's do three of these.

One... two... three...

You are strong like the ocean. You move with the tides and experience life through troubled waters and calm waters. You are aware of others who live life with you and as you take another deep breath you are aware of those breathing all around you, even those you can't see and those who seem far away.

When you are ready, slowly open your eyes and observe your surroundings.

## REFLECTION QUESTIONS

Something that helps me feel calm is ..............................................

..........................................................................................

Something that helps me feel safe is ..............................................

..........................................................................................

Something that makes me feel strong is ..............................................

..........................................................................................

# Mindful sleep

*This meditation will help your child to relax their mind and body before falling asleep.*

Once you are laying flat on your back, close your eyes and place your hands on your stomach. Take a deep breath in and out through your nose while focusing on the rise and fall of your stomach.

Imagine each individual thought in your head as a single cloud and with every breath in and out the thoughts float away. Take a few more slow deep breaths in and out until you are imagining only a clear sky.

The sky is a blank canvas in which you will soon color with hopes and dreams. While you sleep, your hopes will shine like the stars, each appearing as you let your mind focus on the present moment of each breath. Your dreams will come after you are asleep and they will rise with the sun, guiding you on your journey ahead.

Take a deep breath in and out and focus on your feet. Have they helped you walk or run today?

Focus on your hands on your belly. Did you use them to help a friend today?

Imagine your body is so still the only movements can be found in the rise and fall of your breathing and your heart beating. As you fall asleep, your heart and mind will work together to continue your mindful breaths.

# My sleep journal

Today is ........................................................

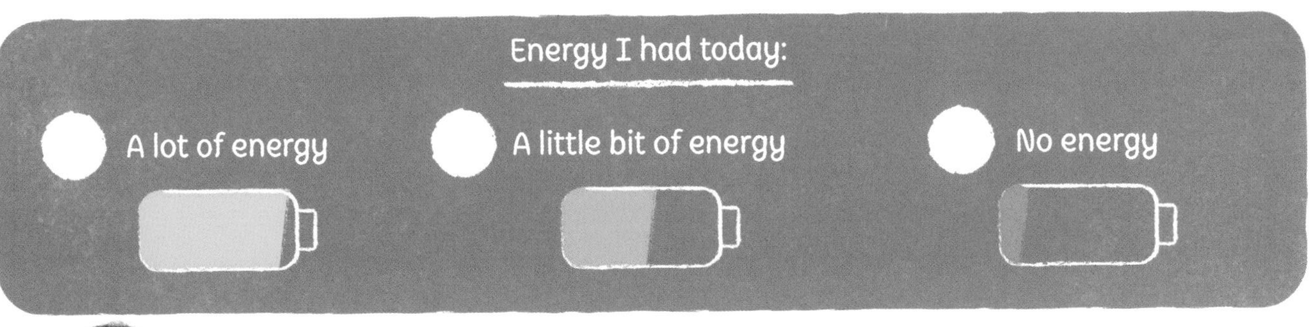

Energy I had today:

- A lot of energy
- A little bit of energy
- No energy

Movement breaks I did today : ...............

## Before I went to bed

Draw an activity of what you did before going to bed

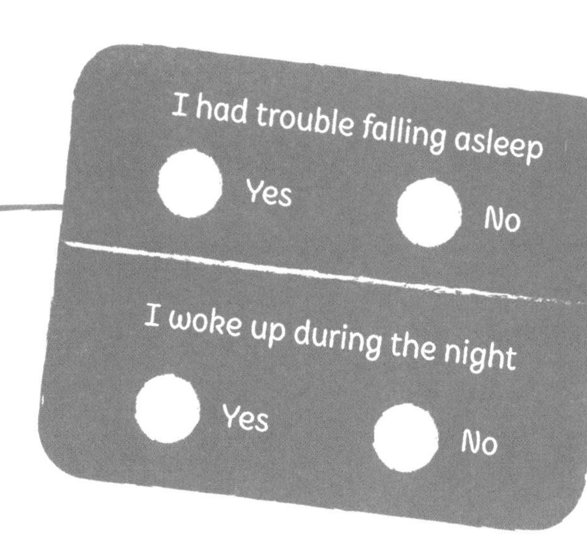

I had trouble falling asleep

- Yes
- No

I woke up during the night

- Yes
- No

I slept for ...... hours

I dreamed about

..............................................................................................

..............................................................................................

When I woke up I felt ..................................................................

# I am enough

*This meditation will remind your child to show themselves compassion. This is a helpful meditation for when your child needs to feel confident and motivated.*

*After each affirmation, there is a space below for you to write the sentence again or to create your own affirmations! You can use these as a reminder to show yourself compassion when you are feeling down.*

---

Close your eyes and take a deep breath in and slowly let it out. As you continue this pattern of slowly breathing in and out I want you to focus on your inner self. I want you to repeat each of the affirmations as if your own heart is speaking to you and comforting you.

Allow yourself to be in the present moment and let your mind clear.
I am here.

.......................

..................

You are capable of the challenges you may face each day.
I am brave.

....................

...............

Even when the days feel long with uncertainty, you are strong.
I am strong.

....................

..............

You are exactly who you are meant to be.
I am me.

.....................

..................

Make your own affirmation cards on page 37!

Your uniqueness
is powerful.
I am wonderful.

....................

................

Your compassion
grows with each day.
I am kind.

....................

................

You are loved
beyond measure.
I am loved.

....................

................

Your smile shines
like the sun and can
brighten anyone's day.
I am positive.

....................

................

You are here: strong,
brave, wonderful,
kind, loved, positive.
I am enough.

....................

................

When you are ready, open your eyes.
Throughout the day we can remind
ourselves of these affirmations.

## Journey with confidence

In this meditation your child will go on a journey in which they face obstacles but are empowered to overcome them through their self-confidence. This meditation is helpful for when your child is feeling unmotivated.

Close your eyes and find stillness as you prepare your minds to focus on your journey ahead.

Slowly take a deep breath in as you imagine the sea swelling with the wind and breathing out as the sea calms with a softer breeze.

Imagine now you are on a boat, with the breeze guiding the sails and the sun warming the surface beneath your feet.

The journey ahead seems long and full of uncertainties but you are comforted by your ability to sail through rough waters.

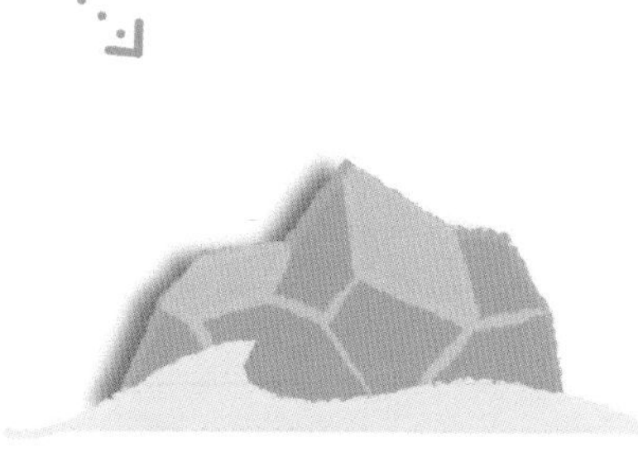

Just ahead of you there is a rock and you begin to wonder if you will be able to sail around it. With each doubtful thought the rock seems to be looming larger out of the water.

You stop, find stillness, and remember the challenges you have faced in the past.
Did you remind yourself it is okay to make mistakes?
Who loved and supported you during those times?

Take a moment to feel grounded in the confidence of your strengths and the thought of each helping hand ready when you need it. As you regain your footing, you look out toward the horizon and see that the rock is smaller than it had first appeared.

There is a lighthouse in the distance and its light provides a sure path for you to ease your way around the obstacle. Each person who has helped you in your journey provides a guiding light. You can see clearly now there aren't any waters too rough or obstacles too large for you when you are confident in your ability to sail on.

When you are ready, open your eyes, smile, and enjoy the journey ahead.

## REFLECTION QUESTIONS

One obstacle I faced was when ..............................................

I overcame this obstacle by ..............................................

A few of my strengths are ..............................................

..............................................

## Finding strength in growth

In this meditation your child will imagine a tree's growth and think about their own. This is a helpful meditation for when your child is feeling angry or unmotivated.

As you close your eyes I want you to think about your posture in your seat. I want you to sit tall, with your back straight and feet planted on the floor.

Imagine your feet are roots reaching deep into the soil, nourished by the nutrients that keep them grounded just as your support systems help you to feel grounded even during times of uncertainty.

Now, imagine you are a tree of many branches. You didn't always have so many, which means there is one that has been there the longest.
It has been there since the tree was young. You also have a branch that has been with you since the beginning. It is the reason why you can regulate your breathing now and control your heart rate. As you take a deep breath, think about your heartbeats and how the two are interconnected.
They both work together to keep you alive.

Let's think about our other branches. We have a few that are the center of our emotions, and help us regulate our emotions and learn. These branches need help to grow stronger. They need us to pay extra attention to them because they are a vital part of our tree!

When these branches grow stronger, as we learn more about our emotions and how to manage our reactions to our emotions, the rest of us grows stronger too!

Imagine if every time we were angry we chose to react by yelling or not talking to someone about it. It would be as if a storm was blowing through, creating tiny fissures in the most vulnerable branches of a tree.

When we use calming strategies for our big emotions, such as taking a deep breath, we can help our branches grow strong and weather any storm!

As you open your eyes think about how you can help your branches grow stronger today.

## REFLECTION QUESTIONS

What is something you recently learned how to do? ................................

.................................................................................

What is something you want to learn how to do? ................................

.................................................................................

What are some of the steps you can take to learn this new thing? ................

.................................................................................

# Holiday meditation

In this meditation your child will reflect on their favorite holiday tradition. This meditation is helpful for when your child is missing someone.

Close your eyes and take a deep breath. Once you have found stillness in your body, I want you to think about your favorite tradition. Focus on the first one that comes to your mind.

When you think about this tradition, who do you celebrate it with? Can you remember the sounds of their voices or how it feels when you all share a laugh together? We can imagine joy as a warm sun inside of our bellies and our hearts. With each happy thought, imagine the sun growing larger and larger inside of you.

Think about what makes your tradition unique. Maybe you can smell and taste the meal you share together, see the decorations, or hear the music. Are you inside staying warm or outside enjoying the fresh air? Our traditions are part of what make us unique and special, anywhere we are and for any occasion!

Remember the feeling of joy growing inside of you? Imagine it is so strong that others around you can feel it too! When we share our joy with others, while celebrating our favorite tradition or any time of the year, the joy inside us continues to grow too!

Take another deep breath, smile, and when you are ready, open your eyes.

## REFLECTION QUESTIONS

My favorite tradition is ..................................................

Something that makes me feel joy during this time ..............................

..................................................

One way I can share joy with others is ..................................

..................................................

## Meditation Journal

Date : ..............................................................................

Today's Meditation : ...........................................................................

Before reading the meditation I was feeling

After reading the meditation I felt

3 emotions I want to feel today

3 things I can do to support me in feeling those emotions

Affirmation of the day

..............................................................................

..............................................................................

## Meditation Journal

Date : ..........................................................

Today's Meditation : ..........................................................

Before reading the meditation I was feeling

After reading the meditation I felt

3 emotions I want to feel today

3 things I can do to support me in feeling those emotions

Affirmation of the day

..........................................................

..........................................................

## Meditation Journal

Date : ............................................................

Today's Meditation : ............................................................

Before reading the meditation I was feeling

After reading the meditation I felt

3 emotions I want to feel today

3 things I can do to support me in feeling those emotions

Affirmation of the day

............................................................

............................................................

Meditation Journal

Date : ..........................................................

Today's Meditation : ..........................................................

Before reading the meditation I was feeling

After reading the meditation I felt

3 emotions I want to feel today

3 things I can do to support me in feeling those emotions

Affirmation of the day

..........................................................

..........................................................

## Meditation Journal

Date : ..........................................................................

Today's Meditation : ..........................................................................

Before reading the meditation I was feeling

After reading the meditation I felt

3 emotions I want to feel today

3 things I can do to support me in feeling those emotions

Affirmation of the day

..........................................................................................................

..........................................................................................................

## Meditation Journal

Date : ..........................................................................

Today's Meditation : ..........................................................................

Before reading the meditation I was feeling

After reading the meditation I felt

3 emotions I want to feel today

3 things I can do to support me in feeling those emotions

Affirmation of the day

..........................................................................

..........................................................................

I AM
LOVED
I AM
UNIQUE
I AM
KIND
I AM
STRONG

I AM
BRAVE
I AM
ENOUGH
I AM
WONDER-
FUL

I AM
I AM
I AM

# ALSO IN THIS COLLECTION

## Congratulations!

Mindfulness is an important skill to learn and you learned new ways to practice throughout this workbook. Practicing mindfulness doesn't have to stop with meditations and reflections as there are other fun ways to practice and learn this skill! You can look back at this book throughout the year and using these activities can help you during uncertain times and any challenges ahead that you may face. If you enjoy games and other hands-on activities you can continue to strengthen the skills you learned in this book by downloading Wisdom: The World of Emotions.

In addition to helping the inhabitants of the Kingdom better manage their emotions, you can find other activities to continue practicing mindfulness and learn new skills in problem solving, empathy, and more! We hope you remember how unique you are and how your emotions also make you unique.

Thank you for meditating with Wisdom!

betterkids

www.betterkids.education



Art inspired by Masahiro Naruse

Printed in Great Britain
by Amazon